The Self-Love Book

A Journal To Heal

Imprint

© 2024 Independently published by
Modern Frame Of Mind GmbH
Baerenstraße 1 | 73035 Goeppingen | Germany

ISBN: 979-8338961001

The Self-Love Book copyright © 2024 by Modern Frame Of Mind GmbH
Author: Elias Baar

Disclaimer: By purchasing this journal you understood that the information provided in this journal is designed to provide helpful information on the subjects discussed. This journal is not intended to be a substitute for medical advice or treatment. Any person with condition requiring medical attention should consult a medical professional or suitable therapist. The author and the publisher cannot accept any responsibility for any loss or claim arising of the use, or misuse, of the suggestions made or the failure to take medical advice.

Cover design by Elias Baar

www.modernframeofmind.com

this book is for anyone facing a difficult time, a heartbreak, a loss, or a change. it's for those who have forgotten who has always been there for you and who will always stay with you. this book is for anyone seeking a safe space, and for those who need a reminder that you already have a beautiful home - yourself.

this journal belongs to:

....

"what is it that you need?" my mind asked.

"myself back," my heart answered.

content

what this book is about

self-love is an essential part of the human experience, yet it is often overlooked or misunderstood. it can be challenging to cultivate, especially when negative emotions cloud our perception. *the self-love book* is designed to help readers comprehend the root causes of their self-doubt and guide them to use writing as a tool for processing and managing their emotions.

by acknowledging and accepting negative emotions, readers can begin to move towards healing and growth. rather than denying or downplaying their feelings, they can learn to embrace them as a natural part of the journey to self-love.

this book provides a comforting refuge for those who feel isolated in their struggle with self-acceptance. by putting their emotions on paper, readers can gain a deeper understanding of the root causes of their self-doubt and begin to develop healthier coping mechanisms. writing can also serve as a form of release, allowing readers to let go of their negative feelings and gain a sense of clarity and peace.

ultimately, this book serves as a safe and supportive space for readers to express their emotions without fear of judgment or repercussions. through the act of writing, readers can learn to manage their emotions in a constructive and positive way, leading to a greater sense of fulfillment and emotional well-being. embrace this journey to self-love and discover the profound joy that comes from within.

5 reasons for the self-love book

1 – it takes away the pressure of constant positivity

in a culture that celebrates positivity, the overgeneralization of "focusing on the bright side" can be harmful. downplaying, denying, or dismissing negative emotions denies the full human experience, prevents overcoming painful emotions, and exacerbates suffering. this journal allows you to embrace your full emotional spectrum.

2 – it's built on psychology

studies have shown that journaling can help reduce symptoms of anxiety, depression, and trauma. it helps you organize your thoughts, express yourself, and deal with your emotions, both good and bad, in a positive, healthy way. this journal is rooted in these principles, providing a scientifically backed approach to self-love.

3 – it's a journal for people who don't know what to journal about

if you're the kind of person who wants to get into journaling but doesn't know when or what to write about, look no further. the self-love book is a guided journal designed to help improve your mental health, perfect for those new to the practice.

4 – self-reflection is the road toward healing

through self-discovery, we can find who we are and whom we want to be. divided into three chapters, the self-love journal allows you to recognize and acknowledge your deepest emotions, invites you to explore your inner self, and ultimately helps you gain clarity on your life's path.

5 – this journal is just for you

writing your thoughts and feelings down in a journal allows you to craft and maintain your sense of self and solidifies your identity. the trick is to keep exploring yourself. close your door when you open this book. breathe, flip through the pages, and be completely honest with yourself. this is your personal sanctuary for self-love.

whenever you are feeling

insecure,

uncertain,

unworthy,

self-critical,

envious,

overwhelmed,

regretful,

self-conscious,

or any other emotions rooted in self-doubt,

think about this book.

how this book works:

1. write it all down

2. rip it out

3. throw it away.

why rip it out *

writing down negative emotions can be a helpful first step in processing and understanding them, but keeping those negative thoughts and feelings around may continue to cause stress and anxiety. by ripping out and discarding these negative entries, you are symbolically letting go of those negative thoughts and feelings, allowing yourself to move on and focus on more positive aspects of your life. this process can help to reduce feelings of overwhelm, anxiety, and depression, leading to a greater sense of mental well-being and emotional resilience. by regularly journaling and discarding negative entries, you can develop healthy habits for managing your emotions and promoting positive mental health.

according to a study, individuals who wrote down their thoughts on a piece of paper and threw it away also mentally discarded the thoughts.[1]

as a result, the negative thoughts become less important.[2]

the physical act of getting rid of them allows the mind to move on to other things.[3]

*supportive articles for extra reading, sources cited at the end of the book

how to (actually) embrace self-love

before we can truly love ourselves, we must first become aware of the areas where we need more compassion and care. this journal serves as a powerful tool to guide you on this journey of self-discovery and self-acceptance. by delving into your past experiences, exploring your current feelings, and envisioning your future aspirations, you'll develop a deeper understanding of who you are and what you need.

this journal empowers you to uncover hidden patterns, identify limiting beliefs, and envision new possibilities for nurturing self-love. through self-awareness, you gain the clarity and understanding needed to cultivate a life filled with kindness and respect for yourself. remember, to love yourself deeply, you must first become aware of your inner world, and this journal is here to help you do just that

prioritize yourself

when you go through tough times in life, it's common to neglect your own needs, prioritizing others and making everything else more important than your own desires and well-being. if you're stuck in a situation like this and want to reconnect with yourself, know that there's so much love within you, hidden and waiting to be brought out. this book is specifically crafted for that purpose. it won't transform you into a new person; instead, it aims to help you uncover the truth about yourself. its purpose is to assist you in remembering who you are and how much love resides within you - especially for yourself.

this book guides you through the process of healing and reflecting on your past, understanding who you are, and who you aspire to become. it serves as a tool for healing from past events, enabling you to evolve into the person you are meant to be. consider this book as your instrument to reflect, grow, heal, and become more than you ever dreamed possible. this book is designed to help you connect with yourself - because all the answers you need are already within you.

limiting beliefs

feeling self-doubt is a common experience; sometimes, others' words can stick with us and shape our beliefs. this chapter is about confronting your negative self-talk and past hurts. write down everything that feels hurtful, then tear it out - free yourself from those thoughts. this is your first step toward healing and self-love, shedding those limiting beliefs.

do you like who you are?

throw it away.

do you miss anything right now?

rip it out and throw it away.

what is the first thing you need
to forgive yourself for?

write it out and throw it away.

what's something hurtful that was said to you
that you still carry with you to this day?

throw it away.

what do you struggle with
the most in your life?

throw it away.

do you punish yourself?

how?

throw it away.

what emotions do you try to avoid?

why?

throw it away.

do you try to hide parts of yourself from others?

throw it away.

what's something you'd change about yourself?

throw it away.

what are your insecurities?

rip it out and wash off the ink
(or burn it. whatever.)

what harsh truth do you chose to ignore
that you know you shouldn't?

throw it away.

are you still you if everyone looks at
you differently?

47

are you still you if everyone looks at
you differently?

throw it away.

what limiting beliefs are holding you back?

throw it away.

what do you still judge yourself for?

throw it away.

what do you still feel guilty about?

cut this page into 1000 pieces.

what baggage do you carry from your past?

throw it away.

write down every negative thought you have
had about yourself, as well as any negative
things others have said to you.

throw it away. that's not true.

who was the first person that made you
feel unlovable?

find a creative way to destroy it.

use this as a letter to someone who
has made you doubt yourself.

what would you write?

write it out and throw it away.

what's the hardest part about being you?

i'm proud of you.

what is something you have
never told anyone?

throw it away.

why are you so hard on yourself? is it your
genuine belief or something others
have projected onto you?

throw it away.

why do you hold those beliefs about yourself?

now throw it away.

what are you overthinking right now?

throw it away.

if you were to stay exactly as you are right now for the rest of your life, how would you feel about yourself?

rip it out and throw it away.

what's the hardest thing that life taught you?

throw it away.

how did your parents fuck you up?

rip it out and throw it away.

how have your parents affected
your views about yourself?

throw it away.

what's the most painful thing someone said to you?

throw it away.

what is something that you keep repeating
in your head?

throw it away.

healing

in this chapter, you'll find a small collection of quotes that explore self-image, self-love, and self-perspective. think of them as heartfelt notes to empower and inspire you.

the self-love book

"what is it that you need?" my mind asked.

"myself back," my heart answered.

you are enough.

you have always been enough.

love yourself

you have been going through a lot. you've been seeking love and validation from others so intensely that you forgot the only person you truly needed was yourself.

never lose hope

never lose hope that more beautiful things can come to you and that you will have a beautiful life, no matter what you are going through right now.

let it go

let it go and trust that something beautiful will grow in its place.

walk away

learn to walk away, and you'll find how to give all the love you wasted on the wrong person back to yourself. when you realize you deserve love without begging or chasing after it, you open yourself up to a kind of beauty that chooses you as easily as you choose it. you attract people who see you for the rare and beautiful soul you truly are.

you are capable

remember to love yourself just as you are, knowing you are capable of achieving great things. keep moving forward, stay true to yourself, and never lose sight of your dreams. you are worthy, deserving, and more than enough.

love deeply

what is meant for you will always stay with you. love deeply without trying to possess or control; let beautiful connections flow through you without clinging. pour your heart into the people, places, and things that ignite your soul. i promise, the right things will stay. you'll never lose what is truly yours. never forget that.

small steps

you don't need to fix your whole life overnight, and there's no shame in being where you are right now. just focus on one small step you can take today to move closer to where you want to be. take it slow and steady. eventually, you'll get there.

new beginnings

sometimes things need to end to make room for better beginnings.

acceptance

you need to realize that the key to getting through the day isn't always about staying positive - it's about acceptance. not every day will be good or happy. you'll have bad days, make mistakes, fail, and mess things up. things won't always fall into place, and that's okay.

live for yourself

you need to ask yourself what you're living for, who you're living for, and if those answers don't start with you, then you're living your life wrong. this is your life, and you shouldn't waste it on dull things or on people who don't understand the love you carry within you. you only live once, and it's your job to make it count. so let every day be yours, own it, and never apologize for being who you are.

you are worthy

if you've forgotten or don't feel enough right now, remember that you are worthy and deserving of everything you want in life. you have unique talents and strengths that make you valuable. believe in yourself and your dreams. you are enough just as you are, and you can achieve great things. trust in your journey and stay true to yourself. you are worthy and deserving.

you deserve love

you deserve to experience love that mirrors your own. you deserve to be truly seen. you deserve to love someone who accepts your journey with compassion, free from judgment or condemnation for how you've coped with sadness. you deserve to be chosen fully, without reservations or half-hearted affection.

you deserve someone who is unequivocally certain of you; someone who remains by your side.

the universe mirrors you

the universe will keep teaching you the same lessons, bringing you the same kinds of relationships, love, and pain until you realize it all comes back to you. until you're fed up with repeating old patterns. until you truly value yourself enough to raise your standards and believe you deserve better.

until you learn to love yourself more, you'll keep settling for love that mirrors how you feel about yourself. the answers to everything you want are already inside you.

things always fall into place

if you look closely at your life, you'll notice that things always fall into place. every experience leads you to a better destination. you grow through every challenge, even the ones you think you can't survive. that's the nature of life. never forget that.

spend time alone

sometimes, you need to spend time alone before a big breakthrough. you're meant to let go of old identities and relationships that hold you back. embrace this time. stand tall and walk your path alone if necessary. this is your time to grow and transform.

learn to love your life

learn to love your life so much that you feel lucky to be you. feel like it's a privilege to wake up as yourself. look at the wonderful home you've created within yourself, the amazing friends you get to talk to every day, and how well you spend your time. appreciate your strong mind and how you take care of yourself. if you haven't figured everything out yet, recognize how hard you're trying and how much you fight for your happiness. how lucky you are to be you.

focus on yourself

focus on yourself. don't let your whole life depend on someone else because people come and go. enjoy your own hobbies and interests. do things for your own happiness, not just to please others. don't wait around or give up everything for someone else. live your life for yourself.

believe in yourself

believe in yourself.

i mean truly believe in yourself. don't just say it - show it. when you're at your lowest and uncertain about the future, take a deep breath and remember that you have had the strength to face every challenge up until now, and that you will also get through this.

i'm proud of you

if no one told you lately:

i'm proud of you.

you're at peace

one day you'll wake up and find yourself in this place. everything feels right. your heart is calm, your soul is ignited, and your thoughts are positive. your vision is clear: you're at peace - with your past, with what you've endured, and with where you're going.

self-love

in this chapter, the focus is solely on you. explore what you love about yourself and discover ways to practice self-love in your daily life. reflect on how the people you cherish influence the way you perceive yourself and how their love impacts you. take a deep breath. flip through the book, stop on one page and write your heart out. those are questions to keep.

exercise

read the following statements and make verbal declarations. repeat multiple times and notice how it begins to feel more natural and a part of your inner truth:

i acknowledge my perceived flaws and recognize that they are part of what makes me unique.

i accept my insecurities and understand that they can be sources of strength.

i embrace my shortcomings and see them as opportunities for growth.

i love and accept myself exactly as i am.

i participate in life fully, regardless of how i perceive my flaws.

why

everything in the universe is made up of energy, which vibrates at different frequencies. when you declare something, the energy of your words resonates within you, impacting the cells in your body. this suggests that the vibrations produced by your declarations can influence your physical and mental state. moreover, the messages conveyed through your declarations also have the potential to affect your subconscious mind, shaping your beliefs and behaviors over time. what adds depth to this dynamic is the crucial role of feeling the emotions associated with your declarations.

in other words: you really have to feel what you declare.

change your perception

you have incredible potential within you. by changing your beliefs, you can change the course of your life. as you release old doubts, something inside you wakes up and moves you forward. your future is full of possibilities. don't limit yourself by thinking this is all there is. dare to dream big, imagine more, and believe in the endless opportunities waiting for you. embrace the universe's potential. think big and live in alignment with your highest aspirations.

repeat this daily:

i am unlocking my potential.

i see my worth and what i can achieve.

i feel the change happening right now.

i sense new energy, showing me that my shift in thinking is already changing everything around me.

what does it mean to you to be loved?

keep this.

who makes you feel good just
by being around them?

keep this.

what are you proud of?

keep this.

what do you need more in your life right now?

keep this.

what would you say to your sister on days
when she is being hard on herself?

now, think about yourself.

write down five positive words that describe yourself.

keep this.

how would you describe the feeling of self-love?

keep this.

what makes you unique?

keep this. especially this.

if you had to pick a song to describe
yourself, what would it be?

keep this.

what do you really need to hear right now?

keep this.

who are you most grateful to have in your life?

keep this.

where do you feel most at home?

remember this.

what are five things that make you smile?

remember this.

what do you think is your biggest strength?

keep this.

what choice would you make over and over again?

think about that.

what is the most exciting improvement
you have seen in yourself recently?

keep (and remember) this.

write down three qualities
you like about yourself.

keep this.

what is one thing you love about your body?

keep this.

how can you show more love to yourself?

keep and remember this.

who has been good for your mental health?

send this to them and say nothing more.

when do you feel most confident?

keep this.

if you could ask your future self about anything, what would you want to know?

keep thinking about it.

what have you grown to love about yourself
that you didn't for a long time?

keep this.

what is a compliment you wish
you received more frequently?

keep this.

what do you love most about yourself?

remember this. especially this.

what do you now understand about
yourself that you didn't before?

remember this. especially this.

who brought back your real smile?

keep this.

what was the happiest time in your
life? what made you so happy?

keep this.

thank you for trusting me and this journal.

it's no coincidence that you've chosen to pick up this book, allowing us to embark on this journey together.

before we close this book together, i have a small request. if you've found value or insight within these pages, i would be deeply honored if you could spare just 60 seconds to share your thoughts in a review on amazon. your reflections, feedback, and experiences matter greatly to me. your words have the power to reach countless others seeking similar answers, potentially transforming someone's life.

tag us in your story on instagram @modernframeofmind, tiktok: @theselflovebook, or send us an email: hello@ modernfom.com

for business inquiries: adina@modernfom.com

i love you, stay strong.

1 Richard Petty: Bothered by Negative, Unwanted Thoughts? Just Throw Them Away (26. November 2012). Association for Psychological Science.

www.psychologicalscience.org/news/releases/bothered-by-negative- unwanted-thoughts-just-throw-them-away.html

February 10, 2022.

2 Sian Beilock Ph.D: Throw Those Nasty Thoughts Away. Physically discarding thoughts we have jotted down quiets mental chatter (16. Januar 2013). Psychology Today.

www.psychologytoday.com/gb/blog/choke/201301/throw-those-nasty-thoughts-away

February 10, 2022.

3 Richard Petty: How to Trash Negative Thoughts (15. Januar 2013). American Counseling Association.

www.counseling.org/news/news-detail/2013/01/15/how-to-trash-negative-thoughts

February 10, 2022.

*supportive articles for extra reading

more books by the author:

"the sadness book" & "the anger book"
now available on amazon!